# WILLIAM YATES'S MAP OF LANCASHIRE, 1786

# A MAP OF THE COUNTY OF LANCASHIRE, 1786

## By WILLIAM YATES

Reprinted in Facsimile with an Introduction
*by*
J. B. HARLEY
Lecturer in Geography, University of Liverpool

PRINTED FOR THE SOCIETY BY MESSRS JOHN GARDNER 1968

# CONTENTS

---

# LIST OF ILLUSTRATIONS IN THE TEXT

# PREFACE

William Yates's map of Lancashire, published in 1786, possesses a two-fold interest for historians of the county. It is, first, a historical document of some local importance, providing a primary topographical source for the late-eighteenth century, but which, half a century ago, William Harrison, a pioneer student of our local maps, reported as already very scarce. This new edition will serve to introduce it to a much wider circle of users, and, if in the past maps have been Cinderella in the family of local records, the Historic Society's confidence in this venture suggests that they are acquiring a higher status. Secondly, the map is a major landmark in the development of our local cartography—a sharp break with the past and fundamentally new in scope and execution. Although William Yates had his successors who prepared similar maps in the early-nineteenth century, by several criteria his work marks the real culmination of pre-Ordnance Survey cartography.

Even in the short essay which introduces the facsimile a number of obligations have accumulated. Particular thanks must go to Mr. J. J. Bagley, Vice-president of the Historic Society, for his persistent and successful advocacy of the project, and for his invaluable advice at all stages. The line illustrations were drawn by Mr. Alan Hodgkiss of the Department of Geography, University of Liverpool, and the original map photographed by Mr. Douglas Birch, Faculty of Arts photographer in the same University. I owe much to their advice and skill, and to the care which the printers, Messrs. John Gardner of Liverpool, have taken with the reproduction of the map. Mr. N. Carrick, Mr. E. A. Carson, Mr. R. S. France and Miss Pauline Round have materially assisted in the search for biographical details on Yates; Mr. J. Langdon of Manchester University has given me information on Yates's depiction of coalpits; while Mr. R. Lawton and Mr. R. A. Skelton have made constructive comments on the text. Mrs. Betty Thomson has kindly typed the manuscript.

The present facsimile is reproduced from an uncoloured copy in the G. E. H. Allen collection in Lancashire Record Office, and at a scale of approximately two-thirds of the original. Mr. Allen, a member of the Society, and the County Archivist, Mr. R. S. France, are thanked for their co-operation. This will be the third edition of the map and probably its largest printing. It may be unnecessary to claim a bi-centenary to justify our venture, but it is perhaps of some interest, that it will appear exactly 200 years after a one-inch map of Lancashire was first proposed in 1768.

Department of Geography,
The University,                                                    J. B. H.
Liverpool, 7.
November, 1967.

## THE ARRANGEMENT OF THE MAP

Yates's map was originally published in eight sheets each measuring $20\frac{1}{2} \times 26\frac{1}{4}$ inches. The sheet numbering probably ran from north to south.

In the present publication the order of the sheets has been altered to fit the book format. Each original sheet has been quartered, but extra sections have been added to depict the Mersey and Ribble estuaries, and the title cartouche and triangulation diagram have been transposed from their original place in the north-east sheet.

The numbering now runs from south to north, beginning in the south-west corner of the map. To make reference easier, the numbers of adjoining sheets have been added in all sheet margins.

Yates's sheets varied slightly in size and met edge to edge. This has made it imposssible to arrange the sections in this book with a uniform overlap. No one regrets this more than the editor.

# INTRODUCTION

## I.  THE MAP IN ITS SETTING

"It is true, *new* Maps of England are daily published; but it is equally notorious, that they only serve to transmit to us the Errors of those from which they were copied, and generally with *new* ones—Sensible of this many public spirited Gentlemen, in different Parts of this Kingdom, have encouraged the taking [of] actual Surveys of their respective Counties, from which correct and elegant Maps have been made on a large Scale. We have thus obtained very good Maps of several Counties, and many more are now preparing . . . " (P. P. BURDETT, Proposals for a Map of Lancashire, 1768).

In this paragraph Peter Burdett, artist and cartographer, and author of an abortive scheme for a new survey of Lancashire, summed up the shortcomings of many existing eighteenth-century maps, and pointed to the remedy. It was to be left to William Yates, a Lancashire man, to construct the first map of the county at the now household scale of one inch to one mile. Yet both these local schemes were the fruit of a tree with national roots. As such they are best comprehended in the light of contemporary cartographical innovations in the English counties at large.

The second half of the eighteenth century was a crucial and distinctive period in the development of English regional cartography. Its history has still to be written, but already it is clear that in concept and execution the maps of this age achieved a breakthrough in standards and helped to pave the way for, even to anticipate, the first maps of the Ordnance Survey. By 1800, the basic maps of nearly every county were larger in scale (at one or two inches to one mile in the main), fuller and more reliable in detail, and had been constructed on more scientific principles, than the county maps of 1750. In Lancashire, as elsewhere, the transformation can be measured by comparing the new one-inch survey by Yates with the previous largest-scale map of the county, engraved by Emanuel Bowen, a London map-seller and "Geographer to the King", for inclusion in *The Large English Atlas*. Bowen's map of Lancashire, dated 1752, did embody some improvements, and the assertion that it was based on the "best authorities"

available was perhaps truthful. Even so, these authorities were maps derived, by several removes, from the sixteenth-century surveys of Christopher Saxton, from the seventeenth-century itineraries of John Ogilby, and from the available charts of the north-west coast. On the resulting map the shape of the county was distorted in east to west extent, its longitude wrongly calculated, and, perhaps most revealing, its larger scale—about three miles to one inch—employed not to insert fresh cartographical detail, but to accommodate a miscellany of historical notes.

Yet, even while Bowen's maps were printing, the first of a new generation of county cartographers was engaged in field survey. In many counties (as later in Lancashire) for the first time since Saxton, a surveyor was attempting an original survey based on mensuration. Several factors interacted to stimulate this activity, but most important the increasing momentum of agrarian and industrial change was rendering the need for more up-to-date and accurate maps especially urgent and widespread. This was nowhere more true in England than in Lancashire. It seems strange, therefore, that the county had to wait so long for a new map. When we examine the chronology of English regional mapping (Figure 1), it will be seen that by the 1780s nearly every county was already served by a new map—and most had been so served for a decade or more. Yet Lancashire was not: why was this so?

The answer will not be found in the general development of English cartography in the third quarter of the century. All the external influences which had impinged on other counties were present to a similar degree in Lancashire. The awards of the Society of Arts for county maps—made from 1759 onwards and a timely stimulus to regional mapping—were universally available. Nor can it be argued that the professional London cartographers, who were keenly interested in the profits to be made out of the new surveys, were any less conscious of the defects of Lancashire's cartography than that of other counties.

Contrariwise, local conditions seemed to favour an early survey. The rapidly changing face of Lancashire's industrial districts cried out

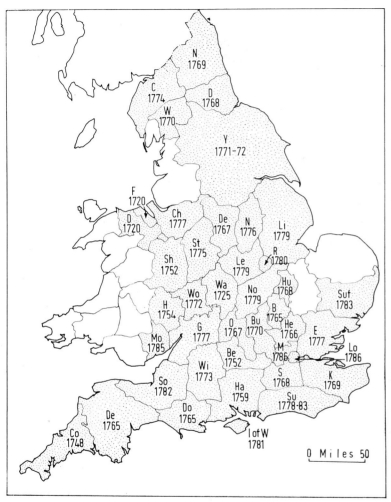

Figure 1.    PRECEDENTS FOR THE LANCASHIRE SURVEY
The stippled counties are those of which a map, at a scale
of one inch to one mile or larger, had been published prior
to 1786.

for an up-to-date map. At the same time, the county was not lacking
in local cartographical skill: a number of its eighteenth-century land
surveyors were clearly competent to conduct a trigonometrical survey.
In Liverpool, moreover, there was a recent tradition (if not a school)
of successful marine cartography. The important survey of the Lancashire coast, executed locally in 1736 and 1737 by Samuel Fearon and
John Eyes, had been several times reprinted, and some of its technical
problems were not dissimilar to those of a regional survey on land.
Furthermore, in Liverpool, unlike many provincial towns, there were
several engravers, such as Thomas Billinge, sufficiently skilled in the
delicate craft of copper-plate engraving to undertake a county map.
The causes for delay in making the Lancashire map have to be sought
in the case history of local surveying projects, and in the regional
support for them.

## II.  WILLIAM YATES:

## SURVEYOR AND CUSTOMS OFFICER

In some ways Yates's survey was a subjective document, as much
a record of personal preference as of fact, so that we need to reconstruct
the environment in which it was conceived and executed. If nothing
else, these biographical facts explain the attenuated nature of an
enterprise spread out over twenty years.

William Yates, on the evidence of age at the time of his death in
1802, was born in either 1738 or 1740. Unfortunately he has proved
elusive in the parish records of the Liverpool district, although circum-
stantial evidence suggests that he belonged to a branch of the local
Yates family, old-established yeomen and manorial tenants of the
Earl of Derby. By the mid-eighteenth century the family had thrived
sufficiently to accumulate a modest estate in West Derby; as well as
being small landowners, some of the family were merchants or crafts-
men in Liverpool. William was a popular family name, and the map-
maker's cannot be clearly identified among several possible baptisms.

For the same reason we know nothing of William's education
except by surmise. His competence as a surveyor and customs officer
pre-supposes a basic knowledge of arithmetic and simple trigonometry,
and his few surviving letters show a command of plain, standard

English. An education at a local grammar school would seem to be probable. But not until his mid-twenties have we evidence that he was acquiring a training as a county surveyor. An advertisement, in the *Derby Mercury* for 1784, of an impending reissue of Burdett's map of Derbyshire first published in 1767 stated that "Messrs Chapman and Yeats" [sic] had helped Burdett with its undertaking. This means that Yates could have assisted in the Derbyshire survey at any time during its stated duration from 1762 to 1767. John Chapman was a competent land surveyor, whose first venture in regional mapping had been a map of the Newmarket District, and he would have given Yates a good grounding in the principles of mathematical survey. Moreover, Yates's training in Derbyshire was probably critical in formulating his cartographical ideas: Burdett's survey, undertaken in response to the premium offered by the Society of Arts, was the second county survey to be successful in obtaining that award.

After 1767, we next hear of Yates surveying in the Liverpool district as assistant to George Perry, former agent to Abraham Darby's Coalbrookdale works, and by then an independent iron-master in Liverpool. Perry had organized the survey for the *Map of the Environs of Liverpool* (1769), on which the help of Yates was acknowledged, but Yates may also have played a part in the preparation of Perry's splendid *Plan of the Town and Port of Liverpool*, published in the same year. Both assignments gave Yates further experience in the trigonometrical techniques necessary for a county survey, and his association with Perry, an industrial entrepreneur, may also have strengthened his conviction that a more systematic treatment of industrial activity on topographical maps was necessary.

Logically, William Yates's next step would have been to make a full survey of Lancashire on the lines of the *Map of the Environs of Liverpool*. If such was his intention, it was thwarted by the decision of Burdett to promote a survey of Lancashire in the fashion of his Derbyshire map, the triangulation for which had already established "the exact Position of a Number of eminent Places in each of the adjoining counties, in order," as he put it, "to facilitate the Continuation and Connection of such County Surveys." In September 1768 Burdett published his Lancashire prospectus and began to canvas for subscribers. In the following year he set up house in Liverpool. Amongst other activities, he quickly established himself as a local surveyor, being engaged, for example, in the charting of Liverpool harbour, and in the reconnaissance of a route for the Liverpool to Leeds canal.

It may, therefore, have been such competition from Burdett which induced Yates to survey elsewhere. He turned to Staffordshire, which, according to the title of the resultant map, he surveyed between 1769 and 1775. However, as will be obvious from Yates's other activities outlined below, it is improbable that he engaged in this survey, even intermittently, for six years. He may have spent a number of field seasons in the county—but that was all. At the same time the venture served to strengthen his professional contacts with John Chapman: *Staffordshire*, again at a scale of one inch to one mile, was engraved in Chapman's workshop, and put on sale in his shop near the "Royal Academy, Pall Mall, London."

Yates returned to Liverpool to launch himself in a new career—as an officer in the Liverpool Custom House: his appointment, as an "additional land waiter" at a salary of £10 a quarter, dates from July 1772. The duties consisted of checking the details of the cargo of arriving vessels against the inventory prepared by the ship's master. Some time before his appointment, by then presumably married, he took up residence at 2, Cleveland Square, in a fashionable professional area, and only a short distance from the docks and Custom House.

Yates still found time for surveying. Matthew Gregson, a Liverpool contemporary, tells us that he assisted Burdett with his survey of Cheshire published in 1777, and about this time, probably in 1774, he formulated his scheme to survey Lancashire. He felt free to go ahead, because Burdett's departure from Liverpool in 1774 had put an end to the proposals of 1768. He decided to go into partnership with John Chapman, continuing a professional association of proven effectiveness. The proposals for their survey of Lancashire appeared in the Liverpool (and no doubt other) newspapers in March 1775. This advertisement represents the blueprint of the Lancashire map and is clearly born of the previous experience of both cartographers.

PROPOSALS FOR PUBLISHING AN ACTUAL SURVEY OF THE
COUNTY PALATINE OF LANCASTER.

In which the true geometrical formation of every place entitled to notice, will be particularly expressed such as division of the hundreds; the situation of market towns, villages, castles, seats and parks of the nobility and gentry; all the main and cross roads, the former measured by the perambulator; noted inns, farm houses, toll bars, milestones, landmarks and beacons, the rise, course and union of every river and brook, and the tracks of all the canals completed or at present intended, will be delineated with the utmost exactness, and nothing omitted that can render such a work accurate useful and ornamental.

As an assurance to the patronizers of this undertaking, that the projectors have no intention of pocketing a subscription without fulfilling the compact, no money will be required till the map is delivered; all that is requested from the gentlemen who are inclined to encourage the design, is the sanction of their names, as a security of being reimbursed the very great expense which must necessarily attend the survey of a county so populous and extensive. The drawings will, with cheerfulness be submitted to the inspection of gentlemen in different parts of the county, thro' the assistance of whose remarks it is hoped that the whole will be rendered as compleat as possible.

BY WILLIAM YATES AND JOHN CHAPMAN

CONDITIONS

I.    The Survey to be Planned on a Scale of one inch to a mile.
II.   The Price to subscribers a guinea and half in Sheets, to be paid on delivery of the map
III.  The work shall begin as soon as four hundred copies are subscribed for; and finished as speedily as the requisite attention will permit.
IV.   The names of those noblemen and gentlemen of the county who are subscribers, will be particularly noticed at their respective seats.
V.    A list of the subscribers, with the number of sets each subscribed for, shall be delivered along with the map.
      As a proof of their qualifications for this arduous undertaking the projectors beg leave to refer the curious to their respective surveys of Essex and Staffordshire, published this present year.
      The subscription will be opened the next assizes at Lancaster.

During the next few years, evidence is scant as to the progress of this scheme; but Yates's other affairs prospered. In the Custom service his advance was steady. In 1777 he was put on the regular staff, and, in April 1778, was promoted to be 'land surveyor' (a supervisory position over a number of land waiters) at an increased salary of £20 per quarter. In addition, he received, on average, £50 a year from the extra 'Fees, Gratuities and Perquisites' of his office. In status he was one of several who stood immediately below the Deputy Comptroller of Customs in the Port. He held the position of land surveyor until his retirement in 1796, and before then had secured lesser posts in the service for two of his sons, Thomas and George.

In 1778 we can again pick up the threads of the Lancashire survey. Richard Gough, the Middlesex antiquary and topographer, had received a letter from John Chapman, stating that he "was engaged with the person who surveyed Staffordshire in a survey of Lancashire," and that it was "nearly finished and I expect to have the drawing by about Christmas." But Chapman died in the following year, apparently without receiving the drawings for engraving. On the face of it we are left to assume that the map was substantially complete by 1779.

As much is confirmed by an independent witness. During October 1780, William Green, a young land surveyor, advertised his professional services in *The Manchester Mercury*: his main testimonial was to have "returned from finishing the survey of the County of *Lancaster* for *Mr. William Yates* of *Liverpool*." We know Green to be a competent surveyor; subsequently he produced an excellent plan of Manchester and later became famous as a Lake District artist. Yates had recruited this able assistant probably to do the field survey. He himself may well have been too busy in the custom service to find time to undertake the detailed topographical survey. No doubt he planned and directed the whole enterprise, and executed the base-line measurement and some of the triangulation, but it is likely that he delegated most of the local work to Green and other (anonymous) assistants. Certainly, in the Custom's salary books there is no record of Yates being granted leave of absence.

The map did not reach the engraver until 1786, six years after the end of the field survey. Again we should ask if Yates was unable to find time for the painstaking task of preparing a fair drawing for the engraver. But there were contributory causes. Chapman's death meant that the finances of the partnership had to be disentangled. And, as will be argued below, Yates may have been holding out for more subscribers. Also, we should not forget that the survey was completed in a climate of commercial unrest occasioned by the American War of Independence. Matthew Gregson wrote in 1781: "With respect to the arts and sciences I am very sorry to say they are but little encouraged in these times of public disturbances." He said book sellers delayed 12 months before settling their accounts probably because the gentry were so slow paying. This depression may have caused Yates to delay publication until local trade had recovered.

After the publication of the map in 1786, Yates projected fresh surveys. Perhaps he came to be regarded as the Liverpool authority on matters of land survey, and, in September 1790, he prepared "A Map of the Line in which the Pipes for supplying the Town and shipping of Liverpool with fresh water from Bootle and other Springs are intended to be laid." His rôle in this undertaking is later reflected in the share he owned in the Liverpool Water Works. He also maintained his interest in regional surveying. Even before the Lancashire map was published, Yates must have been sounding the market in Warwickshire, where he instituted another survey, taken between 1787 and 1789 and published in 1793 by John Sharp of Warwick. This was identical in concept to the maps of Staffordshire and Lancashire. The field survey was undertaken by his sons, George and Joseph, whom he had presumably trained in the appropriate techniques.

William retained his enthusiasm for maps until the end of his life. The copper-plates of the Lancashire map he sold to William Faden, the London map-seller, some time before 1800, but the gold medal of the Society of Arts which it won he obviously treasured. In his will he bequeathed it to his eldest son William, a medical practitioner with the East India Company. To George, who shared his father's bent for county surveying, and was the surveyor of a map of Glamorgan published by John Cary in 1799, he left his surveying instruments, maps, books and terrestrial globe. In middle age he became moderately prosperous. He was able to move out to Low Hill, on the edge of the town in 1779: there he later bought the freehold land from Bamber Gascoyne. At the time of his death he owned his house and its few acres, a second house in Bold Street, and, a "pot works" at Sutton Heath, near St. Helens. But as well as shrewd in business, William was also in sympathy with the cultural life of Georgian Liverpool: he was a member of the Lyceum and of the Liverpool Library, and at home he would play the harpsichord. His wife, Grace, died before him, but of their sizable family three sons and three daughters outlived him. William Yates died in November 1802, aged 62, and was buried in the church of St. Thomas, near his old home in Cleveland Square, and a stone's throw from the bustle of the docks. An affectionate obituary appeared in Billinge's *Liverpool Advertiser*, penned perhaps by its proprietor, a man who knew him well and had engraved his map of Lancashire:

" . . . In the respective situations of a husband, a parent, and a friend, he was an inestimable lesson and example to mankind; for he was tender, faithful and affectionate to his wife; kind, attentive and indulgent to his children; indefatigable in his services, and immovable in his attachment to his friend—His judgement was useful, substantial and profound; acquired by unremitting

application, and approved by experience; always exercised with cautious moderation, not for the sake of ostentatious triumph, but for the information and benefit of those whose minds he wished to improve, and whose acquaintance he wished to cultivate . . . "

## III.  THE PRODUCTION OF THE MAP

A knowledge of the techniques by which an early map was made enables us not only to assess its place in the development of cartographical science, but—insofar as unsophisticated technique imposed severe restrictions on cartographic potential—assists in appraising its reliability.

### (a) Triangulation and the Determination of Latitude and Longitude

The technical criterion which particularly distinguishes Yates's map from its forerunners is that it is based on a scientific triangulation. The theory of triangulation was known from Tudor times, but not until the second half of the eighteenth century, when it became the key to the new cartography, was it widely applied in regional mapping. Surveyors were proud of the technique: William Enfield, for instance, describing the *Map of the Environs of Liverpool*, based on a local triangulation, stated that the map introduced " . . . the *distance* and due bearing of many remarkable and remote objects . . . by a method, which is infallible, when performed judiciously, and with correct instruments." It was still a cartographic novelty when Yates published his map of Lancashire and, following his own practice in Staffordshire, had a special diagram engraved on the map (Page 22). This set down the thirty or so trigonometrical stations and the framework of triangles with their angular values. A note explained that it was "inserted to gratify the curious in Geography; and in some degree to Convey an Idea of the Labour and precision with which this Survey has been carried on and completed." He even invited the mathematically sceptical to check the calculations in the field!

This note and diagram permit the reconstruction of Yates's method. As a first step "two Base lines one of six and the other of ten Miles in length, were carefully measured on the Sea Beach." Since the ensuing triangulation depended on their accuracy, presumably Yates undertook this critical operation himself, using the surveyor's chain as the most accurate mode of linear measurement open to him. Although the location of the bases was not specified, the reference to the *Sea Beach* must refer to the area north of Liverpool, between Formby Landmark and North Meols, a distance of about ten miles, and between Bootle and Formby, extending from six to seven miles. In both cases the site was ideal: not only was it level, but the measurements required no reduction to mean sea level. The Formby to North Meols line seems to have been used as the side of the first triangle, and the second base may have served as an independent check on the accuracy of the system.

The triangulation, designed to establish the precise location of a network of isolated points, could then begin. Yates would have already reconnoitred the potential trigonometrical stations which had to be at suitable intervals, each visible from all adjacent stations, and capable of use in the subsequent topographical survey. Three *principal stations* were selected, probably Billinge Beacon, Pendle Hill, and Warton Crag, judging by their nodality in the whole system. The remainder included other natural landmarks such as Rivington Pike and Coniston Old Man; prominent churches such as Preston, Leigh and Manchester; and windmills, as at Kirkham and Preesall. A small surveying party would trek on horseback from station to station as season and visibility permitted. At each halt they would set up the theodolite—an "instrument graduated with the greatest exactness"—to take readings on surrounding landmarks. Wherever practicable, the three angles of each *great* triangle were observed to help eliminate error. The result was a well-shaped framework of triangles covering the county which compares favourably with the design of the subsequent trigonometrical survey of the Board of Ordnance (1800-1809).

The difficulty of map-making was increased by a lack of accurate data for latitude and longitude. Earlier county maps and marine charts were subject to error. That Yates had sought a remedy is indicated by his map, yet only in an advertisement, dated 1786, does he state briefly that "The latitude, longitude and meridian lines are accurately ascertained by astronomical observation." Latitude he probably computed by taking altitudes of the sun with a quadrant or similar instrument. This relatively straightforward operation yielded the degrees and minutes of latitude, which are engraved in the east and west borders of the map.

More uncertain is how he determined longitude. In essence it had to be reckoned by comparing local time with time at the standard meridian, but Yates does not specify exactly where this lay. On the map longitude is shown west of *London*, but this could imply either the Greenwich Observatory, then being adopted by county map-makers, or another prime meridian such as St. Paul's. Local time can be crudely estimated from the noon-day shadow of the sun, but *astronomical observations* probably referred to methods involving the determination of the meridian transit of the sun, coupled with a simultaneous estimation of local time by an accurate watch or chronometer. From such readings not only could the values of longitude be calculated—depicted in the north and south borders of the map—but also the position of the local meridian line within Lancashire—engraved as passing through Lancaster church and terminating in the north at the compass rose. Longitude determination added up to a tricky exercise in applied mathematics, in which several county cartographers, contemporaries of Yates, had erred. Yates's observations clearly marked a step forward in the establishment of correct longitude. To give but one example, Bowen places Liverpool (St. Nicholas Church) approximately 3° 11′ west, but Yates's figure of 2° 54′ west is much closer to the 2° 59′ of the First Edition of the Ordnance Survey.

**(b)  Topographical Survey**

Yates's account of the topographical infilling was terse. The explanatory note on the map went no further than to state that "the directions and measure of the Roads, the Course of Rivers and Canals, and the situations of the intermediate parts [were determined] by the Theodolite and Perambulator." Two main techniques are implied. First, from the stations in the triangulation theodolite observations were made to fix the position of prominent features in the surrounding countryside. William Green, one of the surveyors, recalls this procedure in *The Tourist's New Guide* (1818): "Warton Cragg," he writes, "was one of Mr. Yates's primary stations for his survey of Lancashire, and from this place the writer angled to all the surrounding country." Secondly, the mapping of rivers and brooks, navigable waterways and roads, and county and hundred boundaries, was accomplished by a series of traverses. Linear distances along the roads were measured by the perambulator (similar to a single bicycle wheel fitted with forks and a handle, which, as it was wheeled along, automatically recorded the number of revolutions), and angles were determined either by the theodolite or the circumferentor (a common compass with open sights). Where traversing necessitated following a stream through open country, linear distance was harder to measure, and, as well as triangulation, use may have been made of a pedometer to count the surveyor's paces. Whether these details were plotted on a plane table Yates does not specify but plane tables were commonly used by eighteenth-century county surveyors. Finally, the instrumental work was probably supplemented by sketches of special features, and, again following contemporary practice, by making copies of existing maps and plans of towns, estates and inclosures. Never before had one survey collected so much data about Lancashire.

### (c) Drawing and Engraving the Map

A critical stage in map-making was the drafting of a final version for the engraver. The draftsman's responsibilities included the choice of map projection, the selection of the scale, a decision on the principles of generalisation, the jettisoning of superfluous materials, the adjustment, where appropriate, for magnetic variation in field observations, and in general the collation of a diverse mass of materials. Both skill at drawing and mathematical accuracy were demanded. With so much at stake Yates was probably personally responsible for the final plotting.

Decisions had to be made about scale and projection. The original choice of one inch to one mile was almost a foregone conclusion. Yates had already employed it in adjacent counties; it was widely regarded as one of the hallmarks of the new county maps; and, moreover, it was favoured by the Society of Arts. Most eighteenth-century map-makers considered projection unnecessary in an area so small as a county, and Yates's concurrence is confirmed by the lack of convergence at the edges of the map.

The drawing would begin by plotting the Lancaster meridian, and then the lines of latitude and longitude. This graticule of rectangular lines would serve as a general framework. Next, the primary points fixed by triangulation would be carefully plotted by the protractor,

after which data from the theodolite and traverse surveys would be inserted. Adjustments were possible at this stage for scale (depending on the scale of the field survey and necessitating the use of a pantograph) and for other factors such as magnetic variation. Material from secondary sources could also be introduced. From a variety of maps and plans details such as the outlines of some towns and the routes of canals (obtainable from both the relevant acts of parliament and from engineer's plans) may have been added. From various administrative authorities, the distinctions between market towns, parishes and town-ships as well as ecclesiastical information, including the rather complex classification of churches and chapels, could have been derived. Finally, Yates gave opportunity for local experts to examine the manuscript draft of the map: "the drawings will . . . be submitted to the inspection of gentlemen in different parts of the county, thro' the assistance of whose remarks it is hoped that the whole will be rendered as compleat as possible." He had left few stones unturned to provide Lancashire with a map equal to the best of its period.

In due course the fair drawings were sent to an engraver, and in this respect, the Lancashire map is somewhat exceptional in its period. It was the work of a Liverpool craftsman, Thomas Billinge, whereas the majority of provincial surveys had been engraved by professionals in the London map trade. Unfortunately little is known about Billinge's career. He first appears as an engraver in a Liverpool directory for 1766; later he became better known as the publisher of *Billinge's Liverpool Advertiser and Marine Intelligencer*. By 1780, when Yates was looking for an engraver, Billinge was well-established in the trade. He was evidently quite versatile because, as well as preparing plates suitable for transfer printing on pottery, he undertook general engraving: a number of his book-plates are known, but, especially relevant, he had cartographic experience. The plates of the 1767 edition of the *Chart of the Sea Coast from Chester Bar to Formby*, by Fearon and Eyes, were "altered" by Thomas Billinge; and he had engraved not only Burdett's *Chart of Liverpool Harbour* (1771), but also much of his map of Cheshire (1777). He turned to *Lancashire* as a master craftsman.

Billinge may have employed assistants on routine parts of the engraving, which was executed in his workshop in Castle Street, Liverpool, but no doubt he lavished his personal attention on so important a local assignment. The drawings were large and had to be engraved on eight separate copper plates each measuring approximately 20 by 26 inches. The process employed was intaglio engraving, using the burin and other tools to cut the detail of the map (in reverse) into the plates which had first been waxed to receive a tracing of the drawings. When the maps were printed, the proof impressions were carefully corrected by Yates himself, possibly aided by Green and 'knowledgeable gentlemen' in other parts of Lancashire.

The map testifies that Billinge was at least a match for the best London engravers. By eighteenth-century standards it is a competent presentation of the data of the survey, and appropriate to the scale and general topographical function of the map. The engraver (no doubt prompted by Yates) broke loose from the standardized and limited conventional signs employed by earlier map-makers: with varying degrees of success, hachures were used for the depiction of relief, and special symbols for industries and different types of vegetation cover make their debut on the printed map of Lancashire. The total effect is one of clarity; although depicting minute details, the map remains legible and generally uncrowded. The lettering is particularly effective and well-balanced, good use being made of different sizes of Roman, Gothic and Italic styles for place names. At the same time Yates allowed his engraver relatively little freedom to indulge in artistic embellishment: a floriated cartouche wreathed the explanation of the symbols used on the map; in the top centre a fine star compass rose indicated the north point; and the title was set beneath trees and the gate-tower of Lancaster castle. Compared with earlier maps its ornamentation was slight. But this was in keeping with a functional map, prepared by a practical man and designed for use in an industrial county.

**(d) Commercial Aspects of the Map's Production**

As well as being a scientific venture, a map such as Yates's was expected to make money. Profitability had not only determined the success or failure of many county surveys, but also the speed of their production, and it is therefore germane to see how the substantial costs of production were recovered. Even before the survey began the costs of printing *Proposals* to attract subscribers, of newspaper advertisement, and perhaps of canvassing custom in the county had to be met. The expenses of the field survey were still higher: skilled sur-veyors had to be retained, precision instruments purchased, and the whole surveying party—surveyors, labourers and horses—maintained in the field. Engraving was another expensive item. For similar maps the estimates of Yates's contemporaries ranged from several hundreds upwards to £2,000 for a county as large as Devon. Moreover, a county survey was a risky speculation. The history of eighteenth-century mapping is littered with abandoned projects, and one prominent London cartographer, Thomas Jefferys, may have bankrupted himself by risking too much in this field. That these surveys had to be financed by local subscriptions, rather than by raising capital in the book trade, points to their insecurity as an investment.

We can see the force of these influences in Lancashire. Burdett's survey was probably abandoned through lack of support: in 1768 he had insisted on 400 subscribers before he would "venture to begin," and presumably, when they failed to materialize, he turned his attention to Cheshire. In 1775, Yates and Chapman entered an identical clause in their advertisement: "The work shall begin as soon as four hundred copies are subscribed for . . . " As to their degree of success, we cannot be sure. Unfortunately "the list of the subscribers . . . delivered along with the map" has not come to light. Subscribers' names were engraved on the map, but, at the time of printing, only about 250 had been collected. Coming after Burdett, Yates may have found it difficult to convince Lancashire that his intention was serious: he had even to reassure the gentry that "there was no intention of pocketing a subscription without fulfilling the compact"; and, at the same time, to waive the usual practice of obtaining half the subscription in advance to meet the running costs of the survey. An advertisement of 1786 sounded a note of anxiety: "That the copy of this expensive, and laborious undertaking may be secured against piratical attempts, the work will not be published till 800 copies are subscribed for."

By the end of 1787 Yates may have calculated that he had covered his basic costs and that the market, if ever, was ripe. The final advertisements began to appear in the December newspapers. The map "in eight large sheets" was to cost a guinea and a half, "or pasted upon canvass, and neatly coloured" £2 7s. 0d.

## IV.  THE MAP AS EVIDENCE

This facsimile edition is a primary historical document, but it cannot be accepted at face value as an unambiguous record of Lancashire topography. Before it can be used with confidence, several questions concerning its nature and reliability must be answered.

## (a) General Considerations

To date the map accurately we must be aware that it embodies data from several different years. For instance, although the title states that it was engraved by Thomas Billinge in 1786—confirmed by the imprint *published as the Act directs, 1786*—we know that actual publication, in the sense of its release to the public, was delayed until the end of 1787. This may be a quibble, but of greater pertinence, we should remember that the survey was virtually complete by 1780, as is clear from statements by Chapman and Green. Collateral proof has to be sought in the internal evidence of the map, and in dating topographical features whose appearance on (or disappearance from) the landscape can be established from an independent source, and which thereby provide either the *earliest* or the *latest* date for the survey. Thus, the Ravenhead copper works, near St. Helens, opened in 1780 but not shown on the map, and the Low Wood and Penny Bridge furnaces in north Lancashire, demolished respectively in 1785 and 1780 but still depicted, help to confirm that we should regard the map as earlier than its published date.

Yates's intention in designing and surveying the map must temper our view of its evidence: we can hardly expect more than its author intended. Statements in the 1775 prospectus, and in the *Explanation* engraved on the map, coupled with what we know about Yates's career and the techniques of map production, assist us in deciding which aspects of the map are most reliable. Two examples must suffice. First, more trust may be placed in those features, such as roads, that were the result of instrumental survey, than in other features, such as the edge of the moorland on which the surveyor is silent. Secondly, we should weigh carefully what Yates intended with regard to settlement: the explanation refers only to *Gentlemen's Seats and Farmhouses*, and the map does not, therefore, present a definitive record. It undoubtedly gives a far more detailed picture of rural settlement than any previous map, but the smaller cottages, which were springing up so rapidly on the coalfields, were often omitted—a fact confirmed by comparison with contemporary estate maps and rentals. This was partly a limitation imposed by scale, and Yates's, like every other map, had necessarily undergone a deliberate process of generalization, selective emphasis and conventionalization. It is a common failing to expect too much of an early map, and then, if it appears to fall short of some theoretical standard, to abandon it as serious evidence.

The potential of the map can only be realized in a context of other contemporary evidence. Of equal importance, only after reviewing the wider evidence for the period—cartographic, printed and documentary—can we appraise its particular or even unique contribution to the understanding of the past. Clearly, in this respect, the map is a composite document. For certain categories of information, such as the distribution of some industries, Yates's map, if not the sole, is certainly the most satisfactory authority. On the other hand, although landowners' names are engraved on the map, no historian would regard this as the best census of the Lancashire gentry in 1786.

Whatever its absolute merits today, it is worth recalling that its eighteenth-century users regarded Yates's map as an exceptionally fine geographical tool. They were, of course, conditioned by the inadequacy of earlier maps, but even so we can profitably listen to their testimony. Particularly relevant is the fact that Yates's *Lancashire* was awarded the gold medal of the Society of Arts: these prizes were not given lightly to all comers. Out of the claims for awards between 1759 and 1809 only thirteen county maps were successful. The Society insisted on accurate trigonometrical methods for the surveys; and the maps were subjected to the scrutiny of experts before an award was made. The Lancashire map was given the usual thorough treatment. In March 1787, Yates wrote from the Liverpool Custom House to the Society of Arts, saying that he had been "informed that the Society . . . have formerly granted premiums for the Surveys of Counties and still continue to give marks of their approbation to such as are executed with precision and accuracy." He had made arrangements to deliver to the Society "Proof Impressions of my Survey of the extensive and populous county of Lancaster; upon which I have been employed for a number of years. It has been executed wholly at my own expense," he continued, "and with an attention that has been honoured with the approbation of many gentlemen of the first character in the County; to whose inspection it has already been submitted, and who have been pleased to attest such approbation by their signatures to the annexed Certificate."

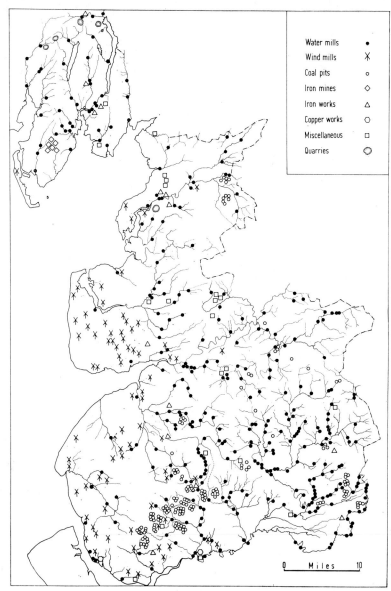

Figure 2. THE INDUSTRIES OF LANCASHIRE
Industrial sites depicted on Yates's map.

Legend:
Water mills ·
Wind mills ✗
Coal pits ○
Iron mines ◇
Iron works △
Copper works ○
Miscellaneous □
Quarries ◉

A certificate vouching for the accuracy of the map, signed by nineteen of the Lancashire gentry, was enclosed with the letter. These referees had found "the several parts within our knowledge, to be a true survey and most accurately delineated." The committee responsible for the award was not apparently satisfied with evidence furnished entirely by Yates; it sought independent witnesses. These reported in April 1787: " . . . Mr. Rawlinson Member for Lancaster being present informed the Committee that in the Map all the parts he is perfectly acquainted with are laid down with great accuracy and the Coast to the Northward is well and accurately survey'd." Mr. Rodes vouched for the parts of the county about Lancaster and Yealand; while the Rev. Mr. Dickenson, also well acquainted with the Lancaster area, similarly assessed the map to "be well and accurately laid down both with regard to the Situation and regularity of the Villages round about." Gentry in other parts of the county spoke up in the same vein. The outcome of these enquiries was that the Society awarded its gold medal. Lancashire had become one of the best mapped counties in eighteenth-century England.

**(b)   The Industries of Lancashire**

As a record of industrial activity Yates's map is especially valuable. The survey was undertaken during important years for Lancashire's water-powered industries, but before the Boulton and Watt engine had made the coalfields attractive for the siting of industry. We can expect Yates to be especially accurate in depicting industry, for not only was he tuned-in to contemporary industrial change, but his technique of survey, involving the traverse of roads, waterways and streams, ensured him encountering the more important sites of local industry.

The depiction of watermills is one of the most useful classes of evidence on the map (Fig. 2). "There is scarce a stream," John Aikin observed some years later, "that will turn a wheel through the north of England that has not a cotton mill upon it;" but only Yates's and similar maps enable the geography of this general assertion to be reconstructed. In Lancashire there were approximately 330 watermills, though not of course all engaged in cotton manufacture, by the late 1780s. The map in effect provides a census. In the floors of some valleys lay an almost continuous tier of mill houses, wheels, dams and

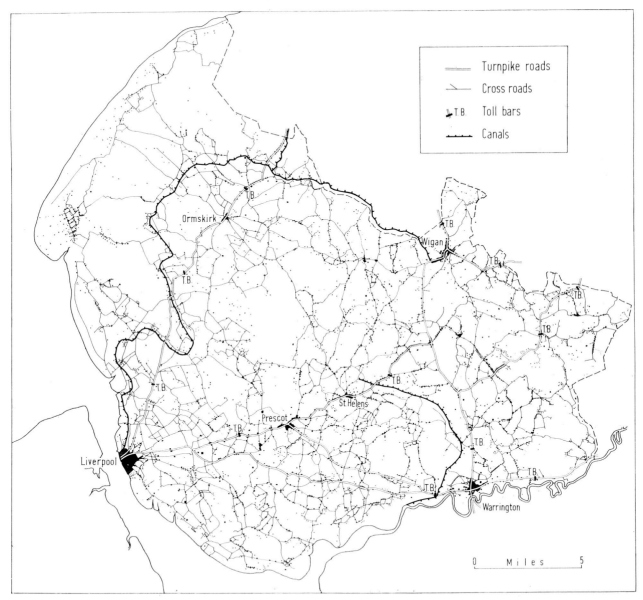

Figure 3. THE COMMUNICATIONS NETWORK AND SETTLEMENT PATTERN IN
WEST DERBY HUNDRED AS SHOWN ON YATES'S MAP

17

sluices: three to five mills per mile of stream were not uncommon in favourable situations, such as on the Douglas at Wigan, on the Irk at Manchester, or on the Irwell north-west of Manchester. The converse of this concentration is also revealed: the waterwheel had already colonized the more remote Pennine steams—as on the flanks of the Rossendale moors—as the competition for accessible sites had intensified. Other sources amplify and interpret the map evidence: water was the source of power for textile processes such as carding, spinning and fulling; in the iron industry it drove the machinery of furnace, bellows, forges, slitting mills and ore crushers; and it was harnessed in the paper industry and in the still important industry of cornmilling. Used collaterally the map is an authority for both the ubiquity and the industrial primacy of the water wheel in the late-eighteenth century.

For other industrial sites it is probably a less authoritative record. Of these only coalpits are afforded a special symbol. Approximately 150 appear on the map, providing a general indication of the active areas in the coalfield. The centre of gravity of mining lay in the southwest apex of the exposed south Lancashire coalfield, in the Prescot-St. Helens area, although after 1774, when the Liverpool to Leeds canal was opened to Wigan, the seams of that area were progressively to undergo more intensive exploitation—a fact which is not really reflected on Yates's map, and fits in with the date of its survey. Elsewhere mining was far more scattered, and its distribution closely related to the water-powered industries of the valleys. On the lower Pennine slopes, and on the flanks of Rossendale, the mountain seams of the Lower Coal Measures and Millstone Grit were worked to supply streamside industrial communities. These general observations may be safely made. On the other hand, it would be erroneous to assume that the map provides an enumeration of Lancashire coal pits. The nature of industrial activity prohibited this on a medium-scale map: many pits were small and scattered and, moreover, often ephemeral. The map therefore under-represents (perhaps considerably) the number of small pits which were worked from time to time in eighteenth-century Lancashire. As much is confirmed when we compare Yates's map with larger-scale mining and estate plans, in the Lancashire Record Office. In some areas, including Shevington, Haigh, the Kirkless area of Aspull and Ince, and the upper Douglas valley sides in Adlington and Blackrod these manuscript plans show pits and collieries unrecorded on Yates. Moreover, in some areas, as at Standish, a single pit symbol

on Yates serves to represent what must have been a colliery containing a number of currently worked and many abandoned shafts.

As a record of other industrial sites the map calls for equally cautious evaluation: while topographically prominent industries may have been noted, others could have escaped the surveyor's eyes. Nonetheless our picture of the contemporary industrial geography is enriched. The iron mines and quarries of Furness, the "limeworks" of the Clitheroe area, the "smithies" in south Lancashire, the copper works at Haydock and Toxteth, and the glassworks at St. Helens and Warrington all emphasise the diversified industrial base on which Lancashire was to enter the age of steam.

The map also depicts the main arteries of industrial traffic. Indeed, as a record of communications, it has no predecessor or immediate successor. Its terms of reference included canals, with locks and bridges, the system of turnpike roads and tollbars, and also the minor or "cross roads." The example of West Derby Hundred (Fig. 3) illustrates the intimate relationship between industry and transport. The Liverpool turnpike, as well as the Sankey and Liverpool-Leeds canals, was essential to the exploitation of the coalfield and its industries. But insofar as these major lines of communication are documented elsewhere, it is as a record of minor roads that the map is potentially so interesting. Here there is no substitute. Yates's survey sets down the essentials of the rural network serving hamlet and farmhouse. We can trace unfenced lanes (sometimes indicated by dotted lines rather than by the continuous lines used for hedged roads) striking across moorland to link valley to valley and mill to mill; and in the plain of Lancashire, the little unsurfaced roads lying between the coastal dunes, or stopping short at the brink of unreclaimed moss. The map does not, of course, record every track and footpath (in the fashion of the modern Ordnance Map) but it is the first detailed record of the local road system.

(c)  The Countryside

What the watermill was for industrial Lancashire the windmill was for the agricultural economy of the lowlands. The distribution of the two types of mill is largely complementary (Fig. 2), although the watermill was commoner in western Lancashire than the windmill in the east. A remarkable chain of windmills covered the western lowlands. There were approximately 80 in all, and in the Fylde alone—still "the

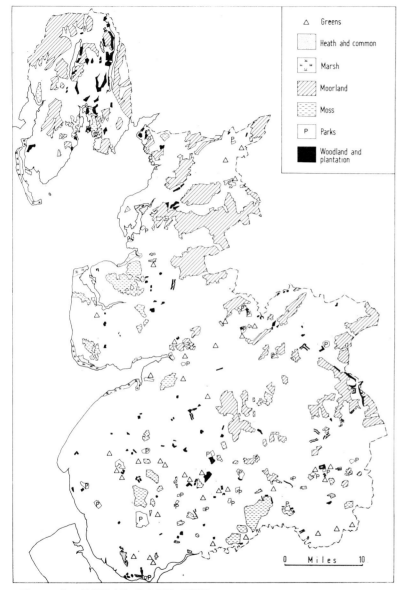

Figure 4. RURAL LAND USE
The several categories shown on Yates's map.

Legend:
△ Greens
▢ Heath and common
Marsh
▨ Moorland
▤ Moss
P Parks
■ Woodland and plantation

0 Miles 10

"granary of Lancashire" at this date—27 are depicted. Many of these eighteenth-century sites are now erased so that the map is enhanced as a record; it is presumably reliable because of the prominence of windmills and their key place in any trigonometrical survey.

To other students of rural Lancashire the map will yield most as a source for land use (Fig. 4). But in this aspect of mapping Yates is less ambitious than some of his contemporaries—no doubt a reflection of his basic interests. The only boundaries he includes are those between cultivated and waste land, drained and undrained, and between woodland and open country, whereas some county surveyors, such as John Rocque the Anglo-French cartographer, had attempted to distinguish several categories of cultivated land. Moreover, Yates sometimes gives the impression of generalizing, rather than showing with true precision the serrated fringe of moss or moorland. This is especially so in the north of the county, where the engraver is somewhat inconsistent in his use of a stipple for moorland and where we are left to infer the limits of cultivation from the presence of hachures, perhaps to envisage a zone where pasture faded indeterminately into rough pasture.

Such caveats entered, the map retains its use as a document in the history of land use. Not only was it the first map to provide this broad view of the limits of cultivation, but such testimony is lacking in other documents and maps. Its conclusions are easy to read. By 1780 most of the woodlands of South Lancashire had been cleared except for timber which stood in parklands and small copses; only in Furness, on the southern fringes of the Lake District, were there extensive tracts of woodland as indicated on the valley sides to the West of Lake Windermere. For moorland and moss, however, the survey antedated the reclaiming fervour of the nineteenth-century. The mossland remaining on Yates's map stands at approximately 34,500 acres—over seven times as great as its modern area. Likewise, some of Lancashire's moors, as in the Lancaster area, awaited improvement in the next half century.

### (d) A Local Agenda

Some guide lines have been set down for the study of the map, but few general rules can be formulated. In the interpretation of early maps as much hinges on the nature of the problem, and the other evidence which can be brought to bear on its solution, as on the intrinsic characteristics of the map. Nonetheless Yates's map is certainly worthy of continuing study at a local level, and two main lines of enquiry would add to our knowledge of its historical reliability.

More detailed local checking would help to establish the validity of the depiction of particular areas and features on the map. Only those qualified in local topography can really adjudicate on the sinuous course of a local stream, the site of a farmhouse, the date of a water-mill, or the bend of an eighteenth-century road. Then again, there are aspects which this essay has not touched upon. How were place-names rendered on the map: did Yates have recourse to literary authorities or are the spellings phonetic renderings of local speech? Are the perspective drawings of churches on the map conventional or are they accurate in their depiction of towers or spires? How reliable is the record of bridges and locks along the canals and navigable rivers, or of toll bars along the turnpike roads? It would be surprising if they were all correct. Such questions and many others remain to be answered from a variety of local sources, including the contemporary maps and plans, newspapers, manuscripts, local histories, and, not least, from surviving field evidence.

Secondly, the map is not a document the sole contribution of which is a static view of the late-eighteenth century. It portrays the county at an interesting moment in its development, but it also needs to be used comparatively. A comparison of industrial sites on Yates, with those on the First Edition of the Ordnance Survey in the 1840s would, for example, reveal something of the changing distribution of industry in the early-nineteenth century; just as those who wish to chronicle the shrinking moss land or fluctuating moorland edge, at a regional or local level, can use Yates as the first of a sequence of maps. Some aspects of the human geography of 1780 can be traced forwards, through such maps as Greenwood's (1818) and Hennet's (1830),and through successive editions of the Ordnance Survey one-inch map, down to the present; for others Yates's map is a salient from which to explore the past. In short, it occupies a key position amongst the total cartographic resources for the history of Lancashire. Although Lancashire was one of the last English counties to obtain a one-inch map, the map, when it came, not only served its own generation well but also gave us in the twentieth century reason to be grateful for the information which William Yates managed to embody in it.

# SELECT BIBLIOGRAPHY

**Abbreviations:** *Trans. = Transactions of the Historic Society of Lancashire and Cheshire.*    *Trans. Ant. = Transactions of the Lancashire and Cheshire Antiquarian Society.*

1. **BACKGROUND TO EIGHTEENTH-CENTURY REGIONAL CARTOGRAPHY**

Adams, G., *Geometrical and Graphical Essays* . . . (1791).

Brown, R. S., "Maps and Plans of Liverpool & District by the Eyes Family of Surveyors," *Trans.*, 62 (1911) 3–34.

Burne, S. A. H., "Early Staffordshire Maps," *Transactions of the North Staffordshire Field Club*, 54 (1920) 54–87; with addenda in vol. 60 (1926).

Chubb, T., *The Printed Maps in the Atlases of Great Britain and Ireland. A Bibliography*, 1579–1870 (1927).

Essex Record Office, Introduction to *A Reproduction of A Map of the County of Essex* 1777 *By John Chapman and Peter André* (E.R.O. Publications, No. 11, 1950).

Fordham, H. G., *Some notable Surveyors and Map-makers of the sixteenth, seventeenth and eighteenth centuries* . . . (Cambridge, 1929).

Gough, R., *British Topography* (1780); also Gough's manuscript collections for a third edition of *British Topography* (in Bodleian Library, Gough, Gen. Top.).

Harley, J. B., "The Society of Arts and the Survey of English Counties," *Journal of the Royal Society of Arts*, 112 (1963–64) 43–46; 119p124; 269–275; 538–43.

Harley, J. B., "The re-mapping of England, 1750–1800," *Imago Mundi*, XIX (1965) 56-67.

Harley, J. B., "The bankruptcy of Thomas Jeffreys: an episode in the economic history of eighteenth-century map-making," *Imago Mundi* XX (1967) 22–35.

Harrison, W., "Early Maps of Lancashire and Their Makers," *Trans. Ant.* 25 (1908) 1–31.

Harvey, P. D. A. and Thorpe, H., *The Printed Maps of Warwickshire 1576–1900* (Warwick, 1959).

Lynam, E., *The Map-maker's Art* (1953).

Ravenhill, W. L. D., *Benjamin Donn A Map of the County of Devon 1765* (Devon and Cornwall Record Society, Exeter, 1965).

Robinson, A. H. W., *Marine Cartography in Britain* (Leicester, 1962).

Rodger, E. M., *The Large Scale County Maps of the British Isles* 1596–1850 (Oxford, 1960).

Skelton, R. A., *Decorative Printed Maps of the 15th to 18th Centuries* (1952).

Skelton, R. A., "Cartography" in Singer, C. (*et al.*) eds. *A History of Technology* IV (1957) 596–627.

Skelton, R. A., "The Origins of the Ordnance Survey of Great Britain," *The Geographical Journal*, 128 (1962) 415–426.

Taylor, E. G. R., *The Mathematical Practitioners of Hanoverian England* 1714–1840 (Cambridge, 1966).

Tooley, R. V., *Maps and Map-makers* (Second edition, 1952).

Whitaker, Harold, *A Descriptive List of the Printed Maps of Lancashire* 1577–1900 (Chetham Society, Manchester, 1938).

## 2. WILLIAM YATES AND THE MAP OF LANCASHIRE

### (a) Manuscript

Lancashire Record Office: William Yates's Will, 26 March 1803; Land Tax Assessment, 1799 (Yates's ownership of a potworks at Sutton Heath).

Liverpool Record Office: Entwistle Collection 11/58, 15/15; Holt and Gregson Papers Vol. 23; 920 SAL 18/7 (purchase of freehold of land by Yates from Bamber Gascoyne).

Parish Registers: St. Nicholas, baptisms, 1778, 8 January, Sarah d. of Wm. Yates Landwaiter Cleveland Sq.; St. Peters, baptisms, 1779, 26 December, Joseph s. of William Yates, Land surveyor, Lowhill and baptisms, 1784, 27 September, Patty d. of William & Grace Yates Land surveyor Lowhill West Derby; St. Thomas's, burials, 1802, 23 November, William Yates Officer in the Customs aged 64 years.

Public Record Office: Customs 18/341–496 (Customs Establishment Books); Customs 39/15.

Royal Society of Arts: Min. Comm. (Polite Arts), 16 March 1787, 13 April 1787; A 14/100.

### (b) Printed

*Billinge's Liverpool Advertiser and Marine Intelligencer* November 1802 (Yates's obituary notice).

Burdett, P. P., "Proposals for Publishing by Subscription A Map of Derbyshire . . ." (1762).

Burdett, P. P., "Proposals for Map of Lancashire, 1768" (Lancashire Record Office, DD He 61/22).

*Derby Mercury* 23 December 1784.

Enfield, W., *An Essay Towards the History of Leverpool* (Warrington, 1773).

France, R. S., "William Yates, Cartographer," *Trans.*, 109 (1958) 200–02.

*General Advertiser* (The) *Liverpool:* March 3 1775; November 30, December 7 and December 14 1786.

*Gore's Liverpool Directory:* 1774, 1781, 1790, 1796, 1800.

Green, W., *The Tourist's New Guide, containing A Description of the Lakes, Mountains and Scenery in Cumberland, Westmorland and Lancashire . . .* 2 vols. (Kendal, 1819).

Harley, J. B., "William Yates and Peter Burdett: Their Role in the Mapping of Lancashire and Cheshire in the Eighteenth Century," *Trans.*, 115 (1964) 107–131.

Jarvis, R. C., *Customs Letter Books of the Port of Liverpool* 1711–1813 (Chetham Society, Manchester, 1954).

*Manchester Mercury* (The): October 10 and 17 1780; January 16 and 4 and 12 December 1787.

Roeder, C., "William Green, The Lake Artist," *Trans. Ant.*, 14 (1896) 100–30.

Roeder, C., "Maps and Views of Manchester," *Trans. Ant.*, 21 (1904) 153–71.

Taylor, H. A., "Mathew Gregson and the Pursuit of Taste," *Trans.*, 110 (1959) 157–76.

*Transactions of the Society For the Encouragement of Arts, Manufactures and Commerce*, VI (1788).

### (c) Maps (including a list of maps attributable to William Yates)

1769, "A Map of the Environs of Leverpool. Drawn from an Actual Survey Taken in the Year 1768. By Wm. Yates, & Geo: Perry."

1775, "A Map of the County of Stafford From an Actual Survey Begun in the Year 1769, and Finished in 1775."

1786, "The County Palatine of Lancaster surveyed by Willm. Yates Engraved by Thos. Billinge 1786."

1790, "A Map of the Line in which the Pipes for supplying the Town & Shipping of Liverpool with fresh Water from Bootle and other springs are intended to be laid." (no copy located).

1793, "A Map of Warwickshire, Drawn from an Actual Survey taken in the Years 1787–1788–1789 by Willm. Yates & Sons, For John Sharp."

1769, Perry, G. "A New and Accurate Plan of the Town and Port of Liverpool . . ."

1803, Horwood, R. "Plan of the Town and Township of Liverpool."

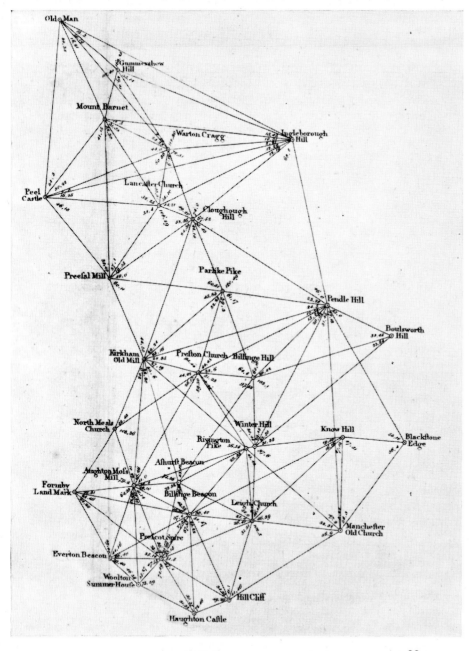

## THE TRIANGULATION DIAGRAM

In the original map this diagram appeared in the north-east sheet, but to have reproduced it *in situ* would have meant splitting it between four sheets. The explanatory note reproduced below was engraved above the diagram.

"The following Process is inserted to gratify the curious in Geography; and in some degree to convey an Idea of the Labour and Precision with which this Survey has been carried on and completed.

That the true horizontal Position of all the principal objects might be accurately ascertained, two Base Lines one of six and the other of ten Miles in length, were carefully measured on the Sea Beach from which Bases (with an Instrument graduated with the greatest exactness) Observations were taken to the most remarkable circumjacent Objects; whose true Situation being thereby obtained, from them a series of Triangles was propagated thro the whole Survey; the most eminent Places were determined by observation of three primary Stations and the directions and measure of the Roads, the course of the Rivers and Canals, and the situations of the intermediate parts by the Theodolite and Perambulator.

The annexed Diagram shews the construction of the series of great Triangles where the circles of Degrees are expressed at each Station which will at any time prove the rectitude of this Map, either to Calculators, or actual Observers."

The diagram is largely self-explanatory (see pp. 11—12), and shows the principal stations, the lines of sight between them, and the angles as measured by the theodolite. Yates regarded this diagram as furnishing irrefutable evidence of the scientific character of his survey, and a means by which his contemporaries could evaluate his work.

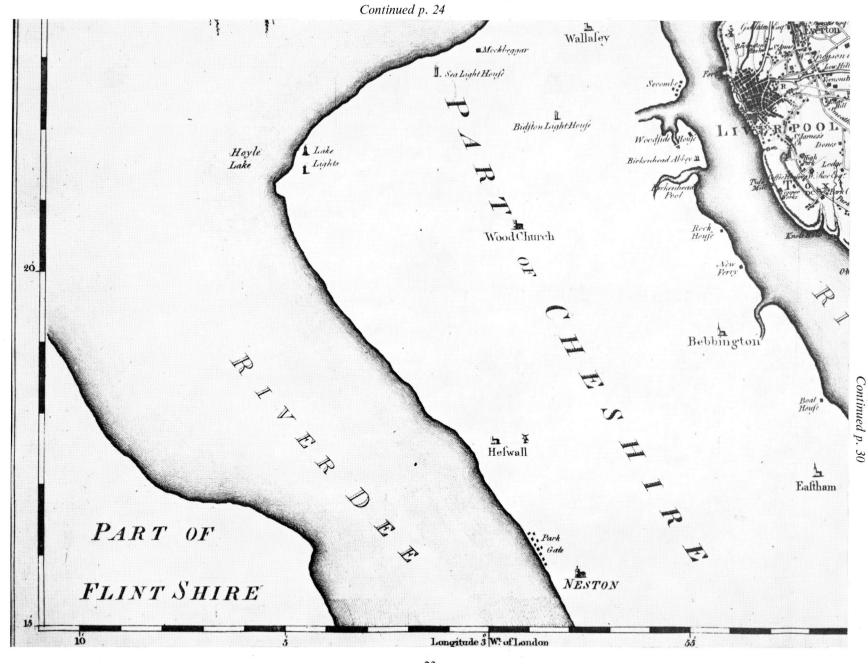

Continued p. 30

Wallasey

Mockbeggar

Sea Light House

Bidston Light House

Secombe

Woodside House

Birkenhead Abbey

Birkenhead Pool

Hoyle Lake

Lake Lights

PART OF CHESHIRE

Wood Church

Rock House

New Ferry

Bebbington

Boat House

RIVER DEE

Heswall

Eastham

PART OF

Park Gate

FLINTSHIRE

NESTON

LIVERPOOL

20

15

10          5          Longitude 3° W: of London          55

## Explanation

Borough Towns which send Members to Parliament, in Roman Capitals ........... **LIVERPOOL**

Market Towns which are not Boroughs in Italic Capitals ........... *MANCHESTER*

Parishes which are not Market Towns in Old Print ........... Childwall

Townships in Roman Letters ........... West Derby

Market Towns and Villages in their true Form ...........

Gentlemens Seats and Farm Houses ...........

Churches and Chapels ...........

Rectory ........... R

Vicarage ........... V

Parochial Chapel ........... PC

Curacy to an Impropriation ........... CI

Chapel of Ease ........... CE

Dissenting Chapel ........... DC

Turnpike Roads and Mile Stones with Toll Barrs marked **TB** ........... TB

Cross Roads ...........

Rivers with Water Mills Engines &c ...........

Canals with Locks and Bridges ........... Lock Bridge

Coal Pits ...........

Boundaries of the County and division of the Hundreds ...........

Continued p. 23

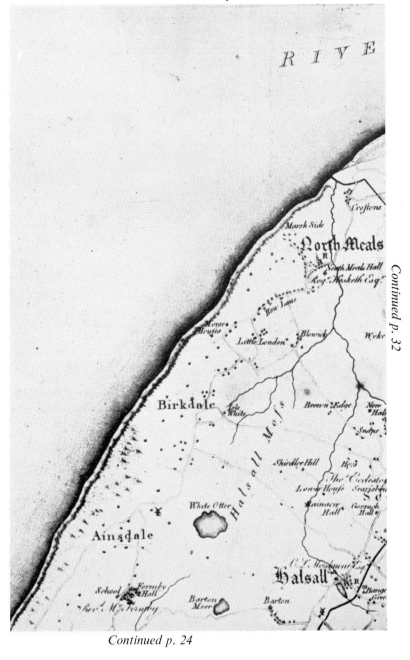

Continued p. 26b

Continued p. 32

Continued p. 24

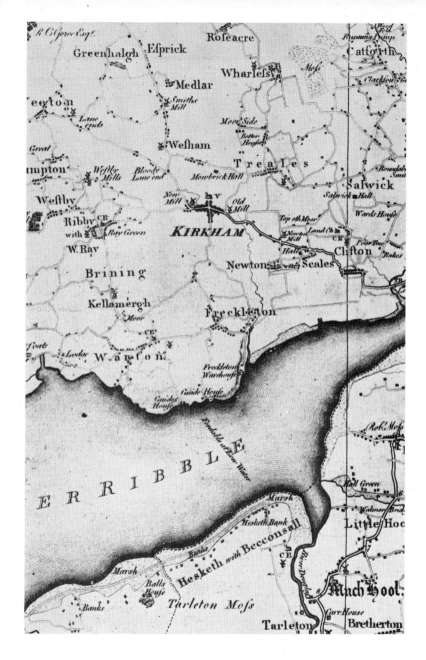

Continued p. 33

Continued p. 25b

Continued p. 28

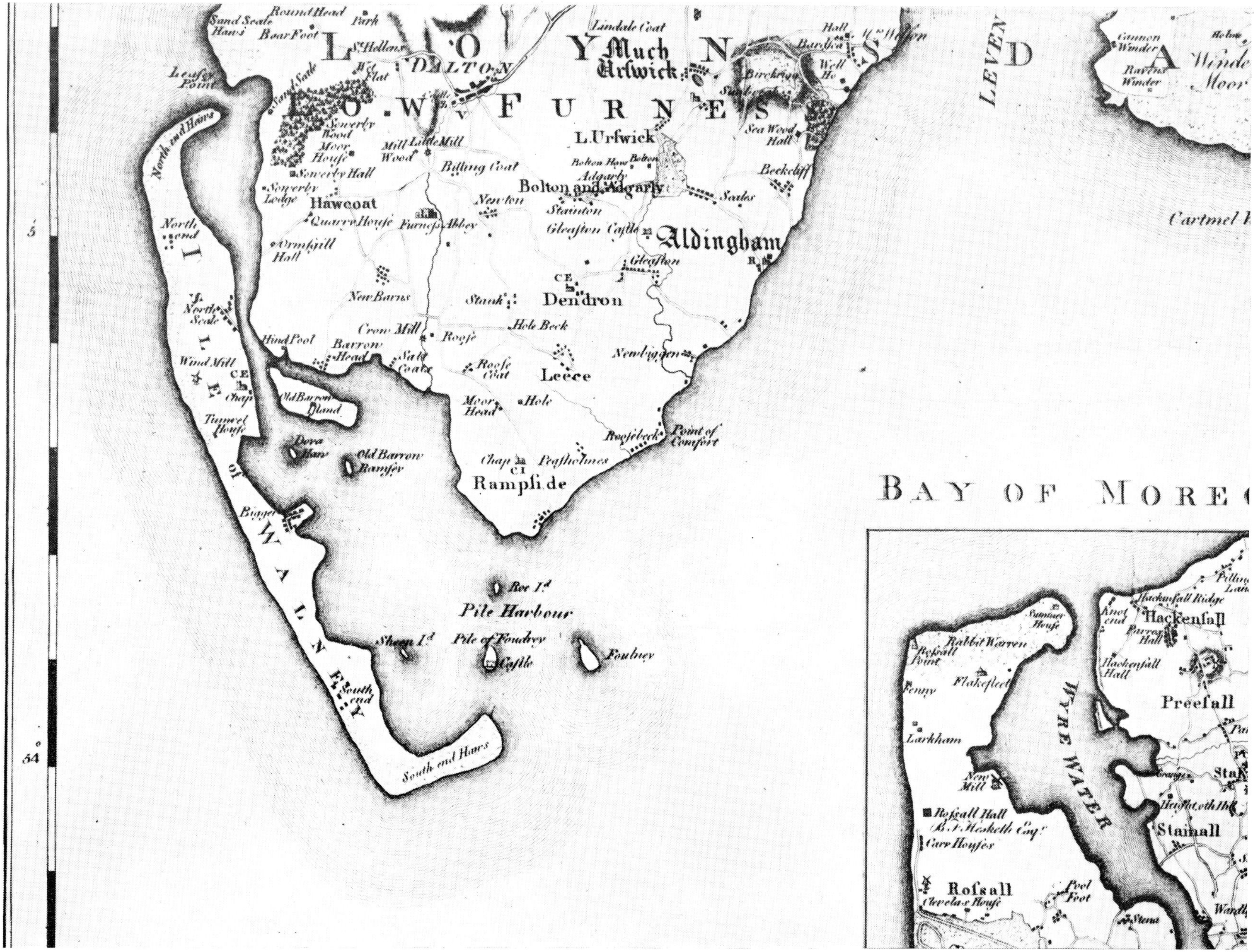

Continued p. 35

LO·NY·N

LOW·FURNES

Round Head
Sand Scale Haws
Bear Foot
Park
Lindale Coat
Hall
Barbick
Well Ho
Cannon Winder
Holm
Winder Moor
Ravens Winder

Leaf of Point
North end Haws
St. Hellens
DALTON
Standscale
Wet Flat
Much Urswick
Birckrigg
Sea Wood Hall
Wr. Watton
LEVEN·D

Soverby Wood
Moor House
Mill
Wood
Little Mill
Wood
L. Urswick
Beckcliff

North end
Soverby Lodge
Hawcoat
Soverby Hall
Billing Coat
Bolton Haw
Adgarly
Bolton
Bolton and Adgarly
Sailes

South Scale
Quarry House
Furness Abbey
Newton
Stainton
Gleaston Castle
Aldingham

Cartmel

Windmill
Ormsgill Hall
New Barns
Stank
Hole Beck
CE
Dendron
Gleaston
R

Tunnel house
Hind Pool
Barrow Head
Salt Coat
Crow Mill
Roose
Roose Coat
Leece
Newbiggin

CE
Chap
Old Barrow Island
Dova Haw
Old Barrow Ramsey
Moor Head
Hole
Roosebeck
Point of Comfort

Bigger
Chap.
CE
Peasholmes
Rampside

Roe Id.
Pile Harbour
BAY OF MOREC

Sheep Id.
Pile of Foudrey
Castle
Foulney

South end
South end Haws

Continued p. 34

Pilling Lane
Hackinsall Ridge
Hackensall
Knot end
Barret Hall
Sumner House
Rabbit Warren
Stekoll Point
Flakefleet
Hackensall Hall
Preesall
Fenny
Larkham
WYRE WATER
Stay
Height oth Hill
Stainall

Rossall Hall
B.I. Hesketh Esqr.
Carr Houses
New Mill

Rossall
Clevels House
Pool Foot
Stena
Wardle

Continued p. 26b

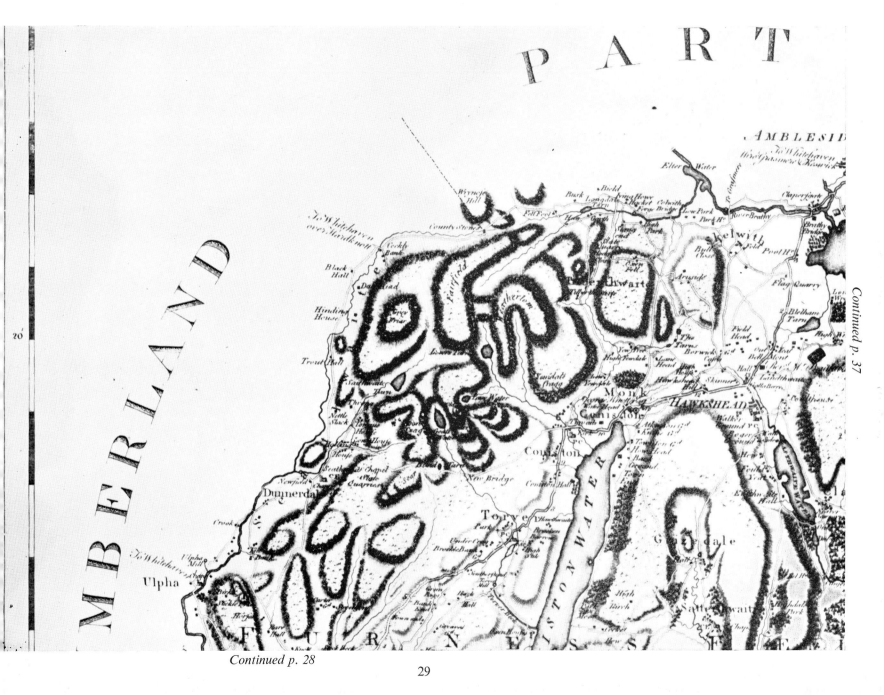

AMBLESID

To Whitehaven over Grasmere & Keswick

Elter Water

R. Rothay

Chaperford

To Whitehaven over Hardknott

Wrynose Hall

County Stone

Fell Foot

Cockly Beck

Black Hall

Hinding House

Grey Friar

Fairfield

Trout Hall

MBERLAND

Dunnerdale

Ulpha Hall

To Whitehaven

Ulpha

Monk Coniston

HAWKSHEAD

Coniston

Torver

New Bridge

CONISTON WATER

FURNESS

Continued p. 37

Continued p. 28

29

Continued p. 23

Burton Wood

Bold Hall

Miſs A. Bold

B o l d

The Old Hall

Slynehead Green

G: Sankey

Huyton

Roby

Whiston

Rainhill

Rainhill Stoops

Bold Heath

Knowſley

Lancaſter Eſqr

Cronton

Crown Heath

Doe Green

Sankey Castle

Childwall

Holt

Torbock Hall

Cronton Hall

Prsc Mill

E. Falkner Eſqr

Farnworth

Hanging Birch

Cuerdley

Penketh

Wavertree

Sefton Park

L. Woolton

Torbock

Hough Green

Upton

Widnes

Peel

Fidlers Ferry

Allerton

G Woolton

Halewood Green

Broad Heath

Little Heath

Ditton

Appleton

Cuerdley Marsh

Garston

Allerton Hall

Halewood

Woodſide

Hale Bank

Ditton Mills

Ditchfield Green

Carters Houſe

Speke

New Hutt

Whitfield

Old Hutt

Burnt Mill

Green

Runcorn

Lady D. Beauclerk

Speke Hall

Oglet

Hale

Hale Hall

Jn. Blackburn Eſqr

Halton Castle

Preston Brook

Staffordshire Canal

R I V E R   M E R S E Y

River Weaver

FRODSHAM

Frodsham Marsh

Eastham

Sr Wm Stanley

Stanley Houſe

Boat Houſe

Ince

Boat Houſe

POOL

Liverpool

Continued p. 39

ORMSKIRK
LATHAM
SHEVINGTON

Heskayne
Clivas Hills
West Head
Bridge Green
Moss
Holland Lees
Standish Wood
Bear Head

Down Holland Hall
Aughton Moss
Earth Hill
Beacon
Stone Hall
Cross Lane
Roby
Gathurst Bridge
Ackhurst
Leigh Place
Wood Houses

Hill House
Lidiate Cross
Down Holland
Hall Welch
Aughton
Skelmersdale
Dalton
Rev. Mr. Holme
Orrel
Walthrew House
Marsh Green

Lidiate Hall
Chapel in ruins
Lidiate
Town Green
Moor Hall
Boulthers
Stanley Gate
Birch Green
Holland
Orrel Post
Narley Trustal
Penberton

Goor Houses
Green
W. Stanley Esq.
Bickerstaffe
Bickerstaffe Hall
Holland Moor
Lawns
Lamberhead Green
Smithy Brook

Peel
Cunscough
Cunscough Hall
Royal Oak
Barron Nook
Moss
Stanley Hall
Winstanley
Goos Green
Banks Esq.
Park Lane Chape

Homer Green
Old Hall
Maghull
WEST DERBY
Rainford
Billing Beacon
Billing
Drummers Fields

Maghull Hall
Simmon's Wood
Moss
Billing Chapel
Simslane End
Downall Green

Sephton
Netherton
Wood Hall
Melling
Red Brow
Parrs
Rainford Mills
Birchley
Blakley Hurst
Chadwick Green
Ashton

Sephton Town
Old Roan
Kirkby
Moss
Mossborough Hall
Moss
Moss Bank
Garswood Park
New Hall
Ashtons Cross

Orrell
Wilbreck Moor
Fazakerley Hall
Little Britain
Windleshaw Chapel
Windle
Garswood Hall
Sir Rob. Gerard
Gerr Mill
Haydock

Black Bull
New House
Higher Lane
Knowsley Chapel
Cadsham Moss
Eccleston
Corkley Hill
Coppull Works
Islands Brow
Black Brook
Crow Lane

Bootle
Fazakerley
Stone Edge
Gill Moss
Croxteth Park
Knowsley Park
Gillars Green
Eccleston Hall
Hardshaw
Yeld

Walton
Walton Hill
Dwerryhouse Lane
Oak House
Stand House
Knowsley
Knowsleys Hall
Ledge
Park Side
PRESCOT
School
Thattow Heath
St. HELENS
Glass Works
Ravenhead
Parr
Sutton
Bradley

Kirkdale
West Derby
Finch House
Wolfall Hall
Brown Edge
Scenter
Sutton Heath
Leach Green
Bold

RIVER RIBBLE

Marsh

Hesketh Bank

Balls House

Tarleton Moss

Banks

Banks

Marsh

Marsh Side

Croston

North Meals

North Meals Hall
Regd. Hesketh Esqr.

Row Lane

Little London

Blowick

Wyke

Midge Hall

Martin Meer

Dry in the Summer Season

Berry House

Mill

Halsall Moss

Shirdley Hill

Hers

Snape

Nerr Hall

Brown Edge

Boscar

Drummersdale

Martin Lane

Scarisbrick

Thos. Eccleston Esqr.
Scarisbrick Hall
Mills

Lower House

Rainacre Hall

Gorsuch Hall

Red Lion

Hurlston Green

Barrinson Green

Martin Hall

Shopcott Hills

Burscough Bridge

Eller Brook

Horscar Moss

Halsall

C. L. Mordaunt Esqr.

Barton

Bangors Green

Jacksons Common

Hurlston Hall

Narrow Moss

Aughton Hall

Burscough
Jno. W. Hitts Esqr.
Blin Hall
R. W. Bootle Esqr.

Latham Hall

Newburgh

Douglass Chapel

Ashton Esqr.

Scarisbrick Bridge
Yewtree

Breakle

Legh House

Blackgate Lane

Meer Brow

Holmes Wood Hall

Sr. Rob. Hesketh

Rufford Hall

Rufford

Old Hall

Tarnscough

Hesketh with Becconsall
C E

River Douglas

Leigh House
Rawstead
Inn
P. Legh Esqr.

Bank Hall

Sollom

Tarleton

Little Hool

Much Hool

Carr House

Bretherton

Walmer Bridge

Hall Green

Moss Side

Leyx Moss

Folds

Moss Side

Little Wood

Lostock Hall

R. Lostock

LEYLAND

Duxwalton
Dukes Walton

Croston
Safse

Parsonage

Eccleston
Bradley Wood

R. Yarrow

Croston Meadows
and Finney

Moss House

Mawdsley

Old Hall

Hurst Houses

Black Moor

Bispham

Harrocks Mill

Harrocks Hall

Fairhurst Hall

Nelson Esqr.

Parbold

Wrightington

Standish

Standish Hall

Moss

Sed Hall

Cliff Lane

Cuerden

Farington
Farington Hall

Clayton
Clayton Green

Old Hall

Leyland

Wm. Faringtn Esqr.

Shaw Hall

Buckshaw

Euxton

Shaw Green

Lickista

Dauber Lane

Anderton
Euxton Esqr.

Peter B.

Astley Hall

Armsriding

Eccleston Green

Caster Houses

Charnock Richard

Wm. Hoghton Esqr.
Park Hall

Heskin

Coat Pl.

Old Hall

Whittle Mill

Neld Whittle

Coppull

Coppull Chap.

Blains

Crooke
Smithy

Chisnal Hall

Hammerton Esqr.

Hill House
Fold

Ripley Esqr.

Mosers Lee

Robin

Langtree

North Hall

Thompson Houses

Meeting House

Quaker Worthin
Burial place

Succession Esqr.

Parsonage

Bamber Green

Continued p. 41

Continued p. 27 inset

Moors

RIVER L...

Downy Field
Stodday
Bailrigg
Overton
Borrough
Brow Top
Booth Fall
Hall
S.t Archibald Hamilton
Bantons
Rendery
Long Moor
Westfield
Ashton
Wads House
Kills
Brow
Yate House
Higher Moor Head
Markett Field
Nan Simpson Esq.
Glasson
New Dock
Conder Green
Ellet Chapel
Cockhall
Dam House Gill
Lower Moor Head
Higher Lee
Sunderland
Pier Hall
O.r R.t Rawlinson Esq.
Ellel Hall
Galgate
Higher Green Bank
Crag Houses
Crag
Lower Green Bank
Ortner
Len Tongue
Foxes
Lower Lee
Donysham
Top oth Emmot
Sunderland Point
Wads Hill
Creek
Gibbon
Thurnham
Smith Green
O v e r W y r e
Leesforth Hall
Chapel Abbey Stead
Emmot Brow
Ranthornthwaite
Moss Hall
Thurnham Hall
J. Dalton Esq.
T h u r n h a m
E l l e l
Catsham
Cocker Sand
Abbey
Thornstnall Hill
Norbrick
Ed. Rigby Esq.
Hampson
Nuthwaite
J. Hinde Esq.
Newland Hall
Dolphinholme
Weir Side
Swainsett Hall
Hillham
Hill House
Batty Hill
Heytorr
Crag Hall
Hole of Ellel
J. Fenton Esq.
Lane Head
Street Houses
Stone Stead
Haysham
Mill
Holleth
Cross Hill
Spout House
Hall
Church
Clifton Hill
Cleveley
Sand Nook
School
Fox Houses
Wheatland Hill
Marsh
C o c k e r h a m
Crooke
Great House
P o r t o n
Cliftons
Sand Side
Above Reed
Little Crimbles
New Hollins
Jackson Hill
Great Crimbles
Hall
Lea Green
Mill House
Hard Head
Har Stones
Lothwaite
Porton Great
Scorton
Moors
Rampool
R i v e r W y r e
Old Hollins
New Hall
Lee Wood
Throstlenest
Faulkners Brow
Barnacre Hall
Sand Side
Pilling Lane
Kirkhams
Pilling Chapel
Pilling Hall
Winmarley
Old Hall
New House
Pere Green
Claughton Hall
Bottoms
Carter Houses
Oakenclough
Hazlehead
Hackensall Ridge
Farrars Hall
Moss Houses
Tyres
Cryststate
Dansons
Hell Beck
Kirkbook
Part of Catterall
Brooks Fell end
Bleasdale
Hackensall
P i l l i n g
Crawleys Cross
Island
New Hall
Linger
Land Scale
High Moor
Brooks Barn
Brooks
Hackensall Hall
Carter
Crawleys Dyke
N a t e b y
Nateby Hall
G. John Esq.
Park Head
Greenhalgh Castle
Healds
Cobble Peacock Hey
Preesall
Park
Bone Hill
Folly
Island
Bowers House
Infield House Butt Hill
Long Field House
Foggs
Pt. Chap.
Staynin
Pilling Moss
G A R S T A N G
Bonds
Battens Breck
Dimples
Sand Holme
Walker Lane ends
Higher Lickhurst
Heighoth Hill
Heskham House
Kirkland
Dandisirk
Stanall
Sowercarr
Hale Nook
Skitham House
Max Butler
Stezacre
Printing Works
Fleet Street
C l a u g h t o n
White Lee
Beacon Fell
Stena
Wardless Chap.
Hambleton Chap.
Rawcliffe
Garstang Church Town
Hall
Catterall
Jos. Brockholes Esq.
Corn Mill
Crimbleshaw

A L E

Cannon Winder

Hobow

Ravens Winder

Winder Moor

Wraysholme Tower

Kents Bank

Hare Will

H U N D

Slack Wood

Leighton Hall
J. Townly Esq.

Yealand Convers

Coat Green

Hall

Docker

Liudeth

Warton Crag

Up Hall

Dale Ho

Priest Hutton

Brown Park

Docker Elbo

Summerthwaite

Snab Green

Borwick

Hall

Warton

Hall

Storrs Hall

Cartmel Wharf

Warton Mill

Caponwray

Moor

LANCASTER

Gnide Point

Over Kellet

Whittington

Gresingham

Carnforth

Church
P C

HORN

SANDS

Thwaite End

Thwaite Yeat

Birkland Barron

Timriggs

Side Garth

Wenning

C E

Mount Pleasant

Nether Kellet

Addington

Aughton

Camp House

T B

MORECAMBE

Bolton Holmes

Hand

Bolton

Lime Kilns

Hilton Moor

Higher Highfield

Middle Highfield

Whinney Hill

Snab

Farleton

Pump Ho

Moor Side

Lower Highfield

Hall

Ch

West Bank

Hatlex

Slent Hill

Westfield

Slab

Llaughton

Hest

Slyne

Ancliffe

Cote

Moor Yeat

Ho

Esq

Cton Green

Belle Mount

Black Castle

Halton

Halton Green

Caton Moor

Bare

W. Bradshaw

Halton Furnace

CE Chap

Folly

Beaumont Hall

T B

Park Hall

Caton

P C

Foulton

C. F. Bucks

T B

Lord Clifford

Forge

Torrisholme

Bulk

Moor Side

Hall

Skerton

Belahills Ridge

Quernmoor Lodge

Quermo

Litledal

Heysham Mill

Crow Dubbs

White Lun

Scale Hall

Pott Yeats

Wittin

Fanny House

Oxcliff

Moss Side

Highfield

Four lane ends

Heysham

Moss

LANCASTER

Gallows

Supress

Beaton

Aldcliff

Bell Vew

Middleton

Heaton Hall

Downy Field

Scotforth

Mill

Longthwaite Hill

Quernmoor

Lawrence

Broughton Brook

Cloughs

Moor

LOYNE

Continued p. 43

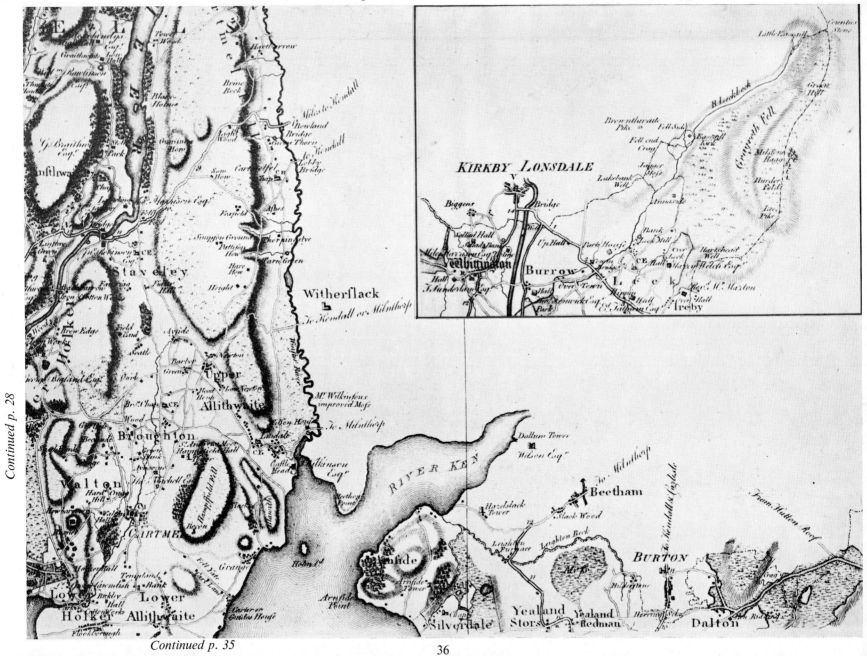

Continued p. 28
Continued p. 35

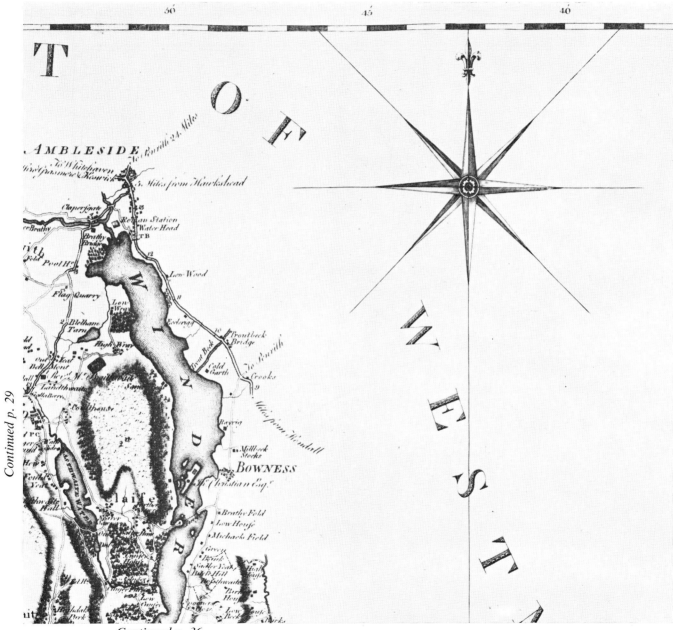

T O F

W E S T

AMBLESIDE

To Whitehaven

To Grasmere & Keswick

5 Miles from Hawkshead

To Penrith 24 Miles

Claperfgate

Roman Station

Water Head

Low Wood

Flag Quarry

Low Wray

Blelham Tarn

Esthwaite

Broutbeck Bridge

High Wray

Troutbeck

Cold Garth

To Penrith

Crooks

Miles from Kendall

Rayrig

Millbeck Stocks

BOWNESS

H. Christian Esq.

Brathy Fold

Low House

Michaels Field

Continued p. 29

Continued p. 36

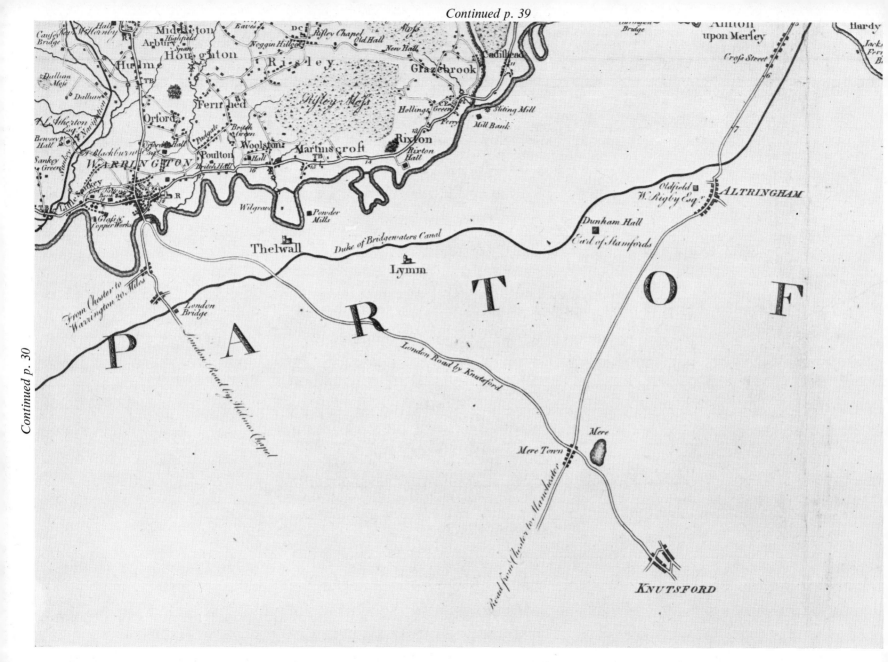

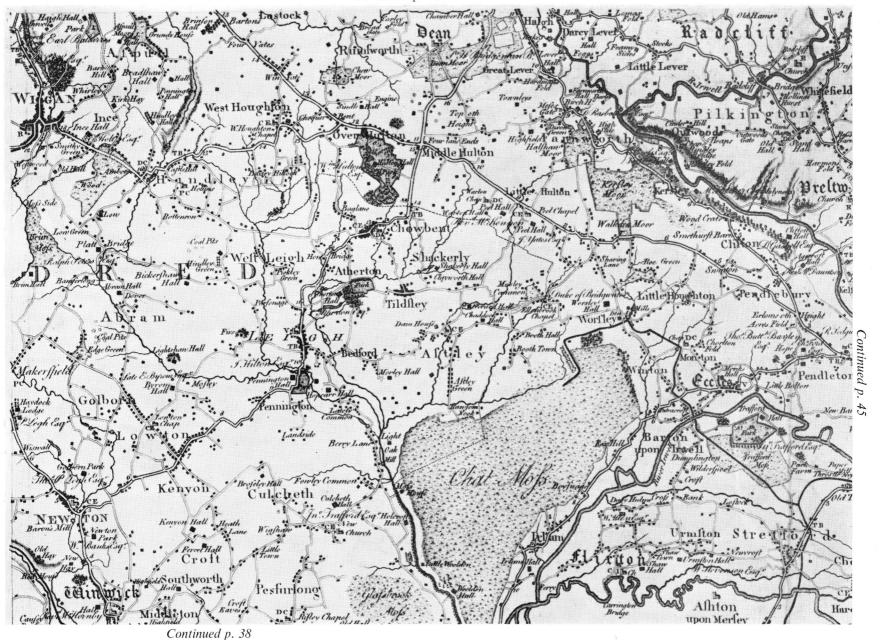

Continued p. 45

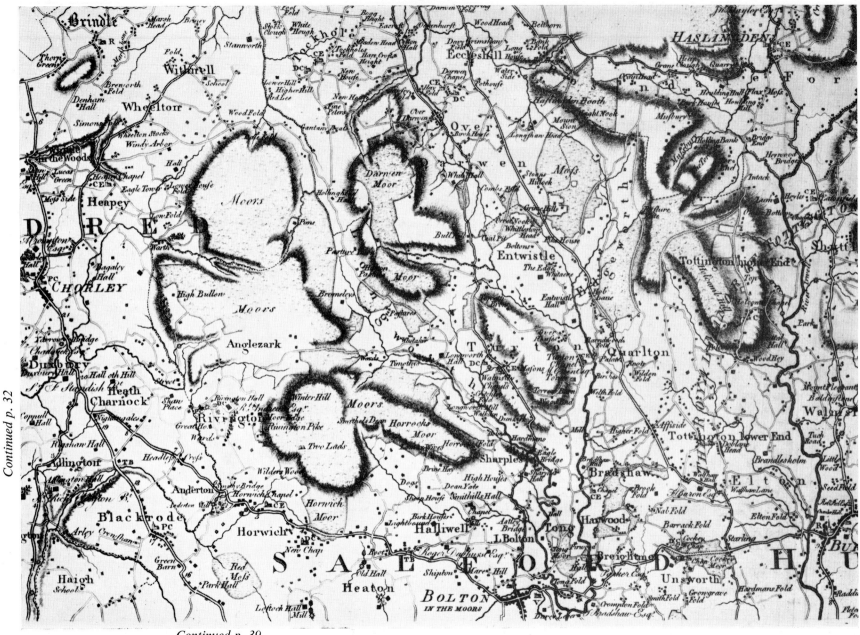

*Continued p. 39*

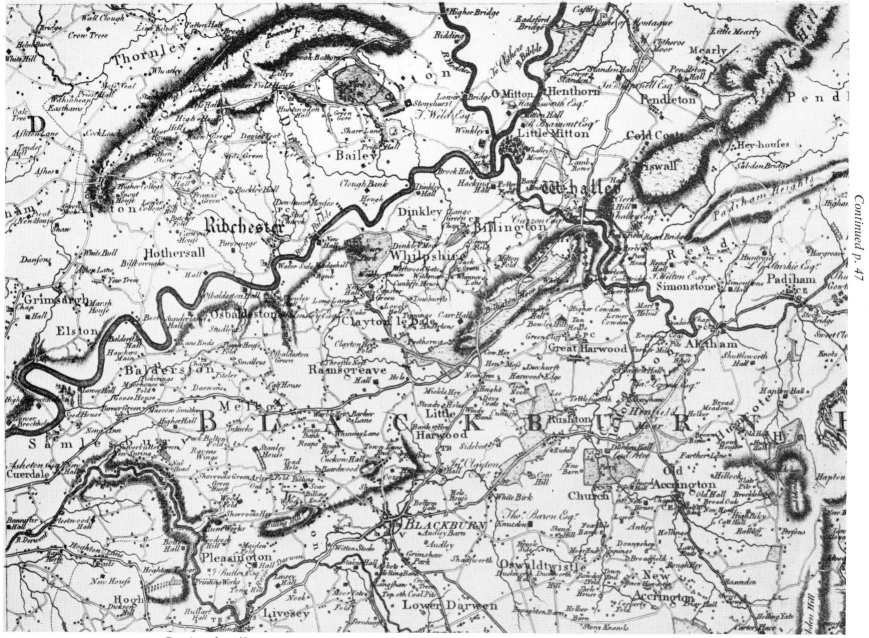

Continued p. 47

Continued p. 43

Bolton Cragg end

Wolf Cragg

T

lighter Side

Tarn Brook

Millers House

Brinan Tarn

Hall

Marshaw

10

Moor

Continued p. 34

O

New Hey

Red Syke

Whitmoor

Burholm Bridge

Fence New

White Well C.E. Chapel

Linklin Green

Fair House

Fairsnape

High Birchwood

Luckhurst

Lower Cromwell

Blindhu

Sadd

Wolf House

Leagram

Smithy Bridge

Downham Mill

Twizal Bridge

Fairsnape

Higher Gor

Chipping Lawn

Harris Ford

DOWNHAM

Lower Gor
Water Yeat

Mill

Worston
Hall

Thorton
Mill

Chipping

Mill

Harris
Hall

Chatburn

W. Asheton Esq

Eaves

Lower Works

Stakes

Little River Hodder

Tw

Barnfield
Brent
Brook

Richmond
Houses

Blackhill

Mytham

Waddow
Hall
Weddal Esq

Lime Works

Worston
Hall

Black
Sticks

Bow Clough
Parsonage

Gibson Bridge

Chaidgley

Lower
House

CLITHEROE
P. C.

Pail

Carr
Side

Rake
Foot

Walker Fold

Holme

Hall Foot

Continued p. 41

Continued p. 36 inset

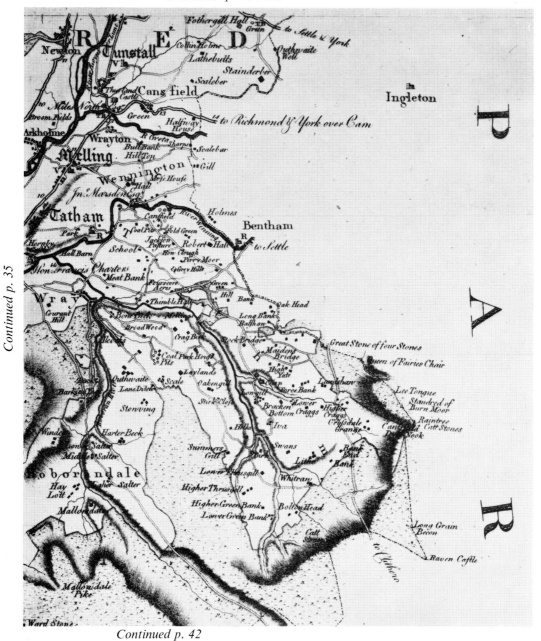

Continued p. 35

Continued p. 42

Continued p. 38

Ferry
Barlow Hall
Green End
Heaton
Wood Hall
Burnage
Didſbury
NORR
S Bower House
Portwood Mill
N Broom Eſqr
Fold
Norr
Hill
Travis Hall
Northenden Yard
Ch
Tep oth Bank
J Phillips
STOCKPORT
Mill Ferry
Ch
Pt
Under Bank
Medlock Abbey
Northenden
Cheadle Bridge
River Mersey
Dale Esqr

GHAM

Cheadle

From London

C H E S H

F

**Statute Miles 69½ to a Degree**

| | 0 | 1 | 2 | 3 | 4 | 5 | 6 |

**Geographical Miles 60 to a Degree**

| 1 | 2 | 3 | 4 | 5 | 6 |

20

15

10              5

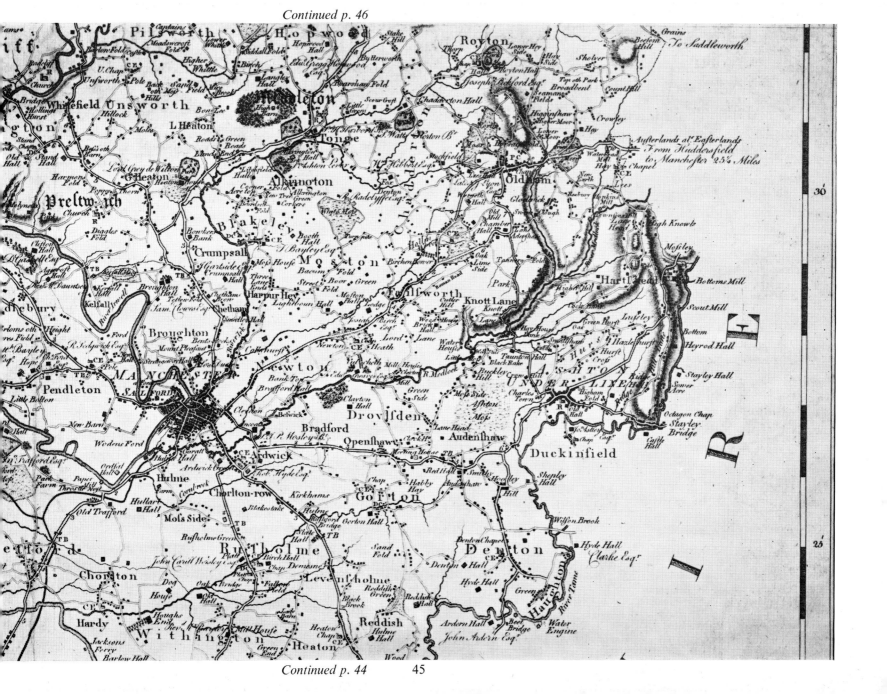

Continued p. 40

Continued p. 45

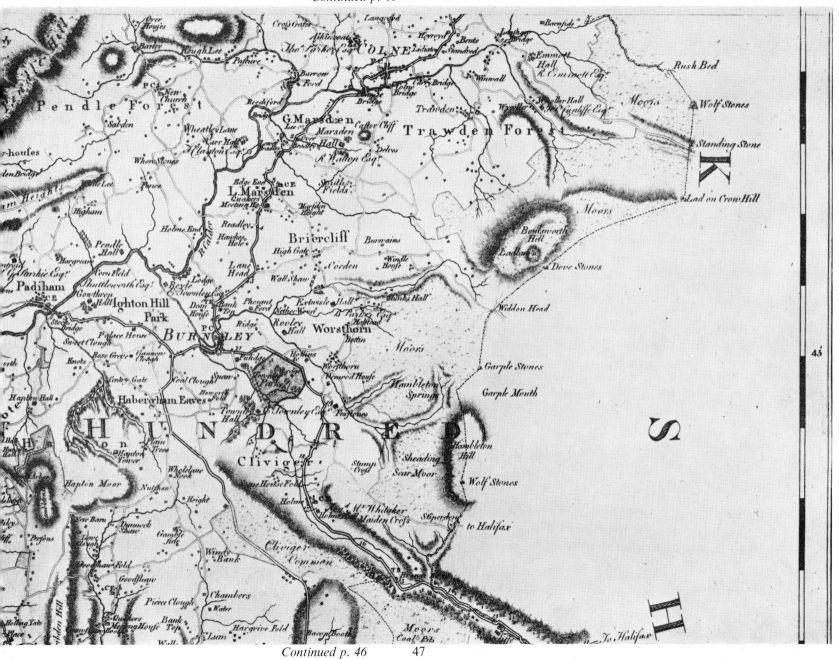

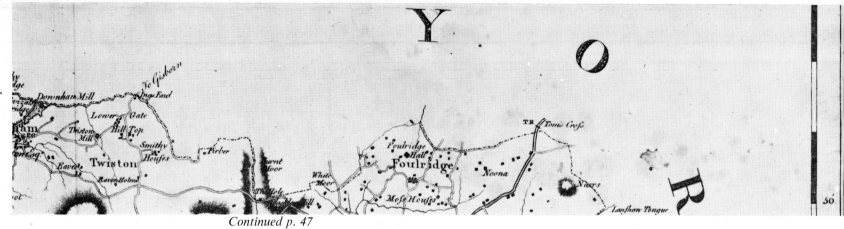

Continued p. 42

Continued p. 47

## A CARTO-BIBLIOGRAPHICAL NOTE

The map here reproduced is from a first edition copy in Lancashire Record Office with the title *The County Palatine of Lancaster. Surveyed by Willm. Yates. Engraved by Thos. Billinge, 1786.* In the sheet margins *Published as the Act directs, 1786* is engraved, although the map was not finally issued to subscribers until 1787. There are no proof copies of the map extant and all the known survivors appear to come from the same printing. The issuing of this facsimile, however, facilitating comparison with a greater number of copies, could possibly reveal further impressions resulting from alterations to the plates while they were owned by Yates.

Before 1800, and perhaps after his retirement from the custom service in 1796, Yates sold the copper plates of the map to William Faden. A second edition appeared in 1800 with *Second Edition. Published by W. Faden, Geographer to His Majesty and His Royal Highness the Prince of Wales. Charing Cross. Feby. 1st 1800* added immediately below the title, and in the sheet margins, outside the border, *Second Edition. Published by W. Faden, Charing Cross, Feb. 1st 1800.* The Lancaster and Rochdale canals (as originally projected) have been added, and the Liverpool to Leeds canal is completed except for the portions which would have come on the lower north-east sheet and the lower south-east sheet of the original map. A number of landowner's names have been revised.

In 1816 Faden issued a re-engraved version of the map entitled *The County Palatine of Lancaster, Drawn from The large Map in eight Sheets, Surveyed by the late William Yates. Reduced by a scale of two geographical Miles to one inch. London Published by Wm. Faden, Geographer to His Majesty and to His Royal Highness the Prince Regent, Charing Cross August 12th 1816.*

In 1840 a further version of this reduction was published under the imprint of James Wyld, Faden's successor, so that the map remained on sale in this form up to the publication of the first Ordnance Survey maps for Lancashire.